W9-APJ-090

Dad's Pizza

Daniel Levine
Illustrated by Chantal Stewart

My dad loves to make pizza.

"We could open a pizza restaurant!" he says.

DAD'S
IZZA

"We would need lots of flour," Mom says.

DAD'S
ZA
FLOUR
FLOUR
FLOUR
FLOUR

"We would need lots of sauce," Mitzi says.

OIL
OIL
OIL
TOMATO SAUCE
refrigerate after opening
TOMATO SAUCE
OLIVES

"We would need lots of cheese," I say.

cheese
cheese
cheese
cheese
cheese
cheese

"We would need lots of toppings," Mom says.

OLIVES
peppers
mushrooms
pepperoni
LIST OF
TOPPINGS

"We would need lots of plates," Mitzi says.

Kitchen

"We would need lots of people to wash dishes," I say.

"I think I'll make pizza just for us!" Dad says.
"Let's eat!"